MW00897228

Connecticut

Revised and Updated

by the Capstone Press
Geography Department

Reading Consultant:
Daniel W. Gregg
Connecticut State Department of Education

CAPSTONE PRESS
Mankato, Minnesota

Capstone Books are published by Capstone Press
151 Good Counsel Drive, P.O. Box 669, Mankato, Minnesota 56002
http://www.capstone-press.com

Library of Congress Cataloging-in-Publication Data
Connecticut / by Capstone Press Geography Department.—Rev. and updated ed.
p. cm. —(One nation)
Includes bibliographical references (p. 45) and index.
Summary: Provides an overview of the state of Connecticut, covering its history, geography, economy, people, and points of interest.
ISBN 0-7368-1231-8 (hardcover)
1. Connecticut —Juvenile literature. [1. Connecticut.] I. Capstone Press. Geography Dept. II. Series.
F94.3 .C66 2003
974.6—dc21   2001047794

Editorial Credits
Jennifer Schonborn, series cover and title page designer; Juliette Peters,
    book cover designer; Patricia Isaacs, map illustrator

Photo Credits
Flag Research Center, 4 (left)
FPG, 26, 28; G. Randall, 4 (right); Ann Troxler, 5 (left); Peter Gridley, 8;
    Clyde Smith, 10; Robert Reiff, 18; Michael Tamborriono, 16
James P. Rowan, 23
Kay Shaw, 30
Lynn M. Stone, 12, 21, 22, 25
Unicorn/Ted Rose, 5 (right)
U.S. Landmarks & Travel/Kent Knudson, cover
Visuals Unlimited/John Cunningham, 32; Mark Skalny, 34

1 2 3 4 5 6 07 06 05 04 03

Table of Contents

Fast Facts about Connecticut

State Flag

Location:
New England
region of the
northeastern
United States
Size: 4,845
square miles
(12,549 square
kilometers)

Population: 3,405,565
(2000 U.S.
Census Bureau)
Capital: Hartford
**Date admitted to the
Union**: January 9,
1788; the fifth state

Robin

Mountain laurel

Largest cities:
Bridgeport,
New Haven,
Hartford,
Stamford,
Waterbury,
Norwalk,
Danbury,
New Britain,
West Hartford,
Greenwich

Nickname: The
Constitution State
State animal:
Sperm whale
State bird: Robin
State flower:
Mountain laurel
State tree: White oak
State song:
"Yankee Doodle"
composer unknown

White oak

Chapter 1
At Mystic Seaport

Mystic Seaport is a busy place. Shipyard workers make wooden boats. Others sew huge sails. Sailors work aboard an old whaling ship. Children learn how to tie sailors' knots.

Mystic Seaport is an outdoor museum. It looks like a town from the 1800s. The museum covers 17 acres (seven hectares) in Mystic, Connecticut. More than 60 homes and shops are part of the museum. So are about 400 wooden ships.

Visitors can board the *Charles W. Morgan.* This is the world's last wooden whaling ship.

Visitors to Mystic Seaport can board the *Charles W. Morgan*. This ship was built in 1841.

The world's first atomic submarine was built in Groton.

It was built in 1841. The *Morgan* could carry 2,700 barrels of whale oil.

Mystic Seaport's visitors learn about life in a whaling village. In the 1800s, Mystic was the nation's busiest whaling port.

The Constitution State

Connecticut's nickname is "The Constitution State." In 1639, colonists wrote The Fundamental

Orders of Connecticut. This was the first constitution written in the United States. A constitution is the basic law of an area.

In 1787, America's leaders wrote the United States Constitution. Connecticut's leaders worked out the Great Compromise. This rule allowed each state to send two senators to the Senate. The House of Representatives would be based on each state's population. This is how members of Congress are still elected.

A Long History

Connecticut started as a colony in 1633. A colony is a group of people who settle in a distant land but remain governed by their native country. Connecticut became a state in 1788. Colonial homes still stand in New Haven and Hartford. A white, wood-frame church stands on Litchfield's village green.

Connecticut is a modern state, too. The world's first atomic submarine was built in Groton. Southwestern Connecticut is home to high-tech companies.

Chapter 2

The Land

Connecticut lies in the northeastern United States. It is one of the New England states. Two other New England states border Connecticut. Massachusetts is to the north. Rhode Island is to the east.

New York is west of Connecticut. Long Island Sound is to the south. The coast of Long Island Sound is the state's lowest point. Connecticut's coastline runs 618 miles (995 kilometers) along the Sound.

Connecticut is the third-smallest state. Only Rhode Island and Delaware are smaller. Many kinds of landforms cover Connecticut, however.

Connecticut's coastline runs 618 miles (995 kilometers) along Long Island Sound.

The Taconic Mountains rise in northwestern Connecticut.

They include mountains, hills, valleys, coastland, and islands.

Western Connecticut

The Taconic Mountains rise in northwestern Connecticut. Mount Frissell is in the Taconics. It reaches 2,380 feet (725 meters) above sea level. This is Connecticut's highest point.

The Housatonic River winds south through the western hills. The Shepaug and Naugatuck rivers flow into the Housatonic.

Candlewood Lake is the state's largest lake. It is an artificially made lake. This lake drains into the Housatonic River.

Bristol, Waterbury, and Danbury are in western Connecticut. They are among Connecticut's 10 largest cities.

The Connecticut Valley

The Connecticut Valley is in the middle of Connecticut. The Connecticut River flows south through the valley. Connecticut's best farmland is located there.

Large cities have grown along the Connecticut River. Two of them are Middletown and Hartford. Hartford is the state capital.

The Eastern Uplands

Several rivers and streams run through the eastern hills. The Quinebaug and Shetucket rivers are long, eastern rivers. They flow into the Thames River.

Many small towns are located along these rivers. Storrs, Plainfield, and Norwich are some of them.

Along the Sound

The coastland along Long Island Sound is flat. It reaches across southern Connecticut. There, Connecticut's large rivers empty into the Sound.

Saltwater marshes line the Sound. They reach several miles or kilometers inland. Gulls and other shorebirds live there. Clams and oysters live in the Sound's water.

Many islands lie off the coast. Mason Island is the biggest one. Others are The Thimbles and Norfolk Islands.

Many important cities sprang up along the Sound. New London and Groton are in the east. New Haven, Bridgeport, Norwalk, and Stamford are in the west. Greenwich is closest to New York. Many Greenwich residents work in New York City.

Climate

Connecticut has a mild climate throughout the year. Temperatures are warm in the summer. The air can be very humid, though. Humid means the air is heavy with moisture. The land along Long

Connecticut Geographical Features

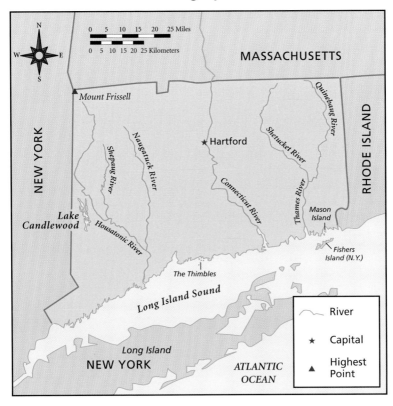

Island Sound has the warmest weather. It is coldest in northwestern Connecticut.

Winter storms sometimes hit northern Connecticut. The Taconic Mountains receive the most snow. Eastern Connecticut is the driest part of the state.

Chapter 3
The People

People in Connecticut are called Nutmeggers. Stories say this name came from Connecticut peddlers. The peddlers sold things door-to-door many years ago. They sold small pieces of wood claiming they were nutmegs. Nutmeg is a spice.

Today, Connecticut has a large urban population. About 80 percent of Nutmeggers live in or near cities. Hartford, Waterbury, and Danbury are large population centers. Many Nutmeggers also live between Greenwich and New Haven.

About 80 percent of Nutmeggers live in or near cities such as Hartford.

Nutmeggers live close together. Only three states have more persons per square mile or square kilometer.

Nutmeggers also live close together. Connecticut has about 657 persons per square mile (254 per square kilometer). Only three states have more persons per square mile. They are Rhode Island, New Jersey, and Massachusetts.

Unlike most states, Connecticut is losing people. In the early 1990s, about 15,000 Nutmeggers moved away. Many left to find jobs. They moved to southern or southwestern states.

Connecticut's Largest Population Group

About 82 percent of Connecticut's people have European or Canadian backgrounds. English people came from Massachusetts in the 1600s. Irish and German people arrived in the 1800s. French Canadians also moved into Connecticut. Italians and Poles came in the early 1900s.

Today, Italian Americans make up Connecticut's largest ethnic group. New Haven and Hartford have large Italian neighborhoods.

African Americans

African Americans have lived in Connecticut since the 1640s. Many of the first African Americans were slaves. They worked on their owners' farms. They also worked in fishing, lumbering, and shipbuilding.

Slavery ended in Connecticut in 1848. By 1860, about 8,500 free African Americans lived there.

Today, African Americans make up about 9 percent of Connecticut's population. Most African Americans live in Connecticut's cities. Hartford, New Haven, and Bridgeport have large African-American neighborhoods.

Hispanic Americans

Hispanic Americans form about 9 percent of Connecticut's population. Hispanics speak Spanish or have Spanish-speaking backgrounds.

Puerto Ricans make up Connecticut's largest Hispanic group. Many others have immigrated from Colombia, Cuba, and Jamaica. To immigrate means to come to a new land to settle. Some Hispanic Americans came from Mexico.

Most of Connecticut's Hispanics live in cities. Many work in factories. Some Hispanic Americans own small shops.

Asian Americans

Connecticut's fastest-growing ethnic group is the Asian Americans. About 82,000 Asian Americans live there. The majority of Connecticut's Asian Americans have Chinese or Indian backgrounds.

Native Americans

Native Americans make up Connecticut's smallest ethnic group. About 10,200 Native Americans live in the state. Most of them are Pequot or Mohegan.

Mohawk State Forest is in northwestern Connecticut.

Two reservations are in Connecticut. A reservation is land set aside for use by Native Americans. The Mashantucket Pequot Reservation is near Ledyard. The Pequot built a huge casino on their land. A casino is a place to gamble. The casino provides money for the reservation.

The Mohegans received reservation land in 1996. It is near Uncasville. Uncas formed the Mohegans in 1637. He was their first chief.

Chapter 4

Connecticut History

The first people reached Connecticut about 10,000 years ago. By the 1600s, several Native American groups lived there. The Pequots were the largest group. They built villages in the southeast. Other Native Americans included the Nipmuc, Podunk, and Quinnipiac.

Dutch Explorers and English Colonists

Adriaen Block was a Dutch explorer. He explored the Connecticut Valley in 1614.

In 1633, English colonists arrived in Connecticut. They came from Massachusetts. These colonists settled in the Connecticut Valley.

Adriaen Block explored the Connecticut Valley in 1614.

They were looking for good farmland. They also wanted to worship in their own way.

The colonists built Windsor, Wethersfield, and Hartford. In 1636, the towns joined together. They became the Connecticut Colony.

At first, the Native Americans helped the colonists. But eventually, the two groups began to disagree. The Pequot War broke out in 1636. Uncas, one Pequot leader, formed the Mohegan tribe and sided with the colonists. In 1637, the colonists defeated the Pequots.

In 1638, more colonists moved to Connecticut from Massachusetts. They settled along the Long Island Sound. Their towns were part of the New Haven Colony.

In 1665, the New Haven and Connecticut colonies joined together. The colonists had their own government. England had little power over them.

The Revolutionary War
By the 1760s, England, now called Great Britain, had 13 American colonies. The English government started to heavily tax the colonists.

Uncas Lake is named after the famous Mohegan leader.

Textile mills helped make goods for the new nation.

In 1775, Connecticut joined the other colonies. They fought against Great Britain's army in the Revolutionary War (1775-1783).

British troops burned towns in the Connecticut Valley. They raided coastal towns. Connecticut sent food, guns, and ships to the colonial forces. The colonists won the war. The United States became its own country.

Connecticut's leaders helped write the United States Constitution. Connecticut approved this Constitution and became the fifth state in 1788.

A Manufacturing State

Connecticut's factories made goods for the new nation. Textile mills spun cotton and wool into cloth. Other factories made shoes, clocks, and tools. Many other goods also came from Connecticut's factories.

The factories helped the North win the Civil War (1861-1865). Companies in Hartford and New Haven sent guns. Factories in Enfield sent gunpowder.

Boom Years and World War I

Connecticut's manufacturing efforts grew even more in the early 1900s. Thousands of European immigrants came to the state. They made goods in Connecticut's factories.

Shipping increased in Connecticut's port cities. Raw materials entered New Haven, Bridgeport, and New London. Finished goods left these cities. They were sold throughout the United States.

Many Nutmeggers ride commuter trains to New York.

In 1917, the United States entered World War I (1914-1918). Troops fighting for the United States needed guns, clothing, and food. Connecticut helped supply them.

The Great Depression and World War II
The Great Depression (1929-1939) hit the entire United States. Many Connecticut factories closed down. Thousands of Nutmeggers lost their jobs.

In 1941, the United States entered World War II (1939-1945). Connecticut again helped supply U.S. troops. The state also made submarines and airplane engines.

Modern Connecticut

After the war, thousands of New Yorkers moved to Connecticut. They bought homes near its southwestern cities. These Nutmeggers continued to work in New York City. They rode special commuter trains each day. A commuter is someone who lives in one city but travels to another to work.

Interstate Highway 95 also helped them get to work. It linked cities along the Sound with New York City. Many high-tech companies built offices near this highway.

In the 1980s and 1990s, several companies left Connecticut. Many Nutmeggers lost their jobs. Crime increased in Connecticut's big cities. Their schools were doing poorly, too.

Connecticut is still a great manufacturing state, however. It is also one of the nation's wealthiest states. Connecticut's leaders are now finding ways to make city life better.

Chapter 5

Connecticut Business

Connecticut has many kinds of businesses. They help the state's economy grow.

Service businesses make up the biggest part of Connecticut's economy. Manufacturing ranks second. Agriculture plays a smaller part in Connecticut's economy.

Service Industries

Insurance companies are important Connecticut service businesses. More than 50 insurance companies are based in or near Hartford. They sell insurance policies throughout the country. An insurance policy is a written agreement that

More than 50 insurance companies are based in the Hartford area.

The Mark Twain house is part of the tourism business.

promises to pay for a future loss or hardship. Hartford is known as the Insurance Capital of the World.

Trade is another big service business. Most trade happens in Connecticut's port cities. They are Bridgeport, New Haven, and New London.

Many Nutmeggers work in tourism. They have jobs in restaurants and hotels. They serve Connecticut's visitors. Visitors spend about $4 billion in Connecticut each year.

Manufacturing

Connecticut has been a manufacturing state since the 1700s. Some factories still make watches, clocks, and tools.

Since the 1950s, Connecticut's manufacturing has changed. Now, aircraft parts are made there. Groton is a center for building nuclear-powered submarines. Computers and printing machines have become leading goods, too.

New Haven workers make tools for scientists and doctors. In New Britain, workers make hardware. This includes nuts, bolts, and washers.

Agriculture

Most of Connecticut's farms are in the Connecticut River Valley. Apples, pears, and blueberries grow in the area. Farmers also raise tobacco. It is used to make cigar wrappers.

Shrubs and flower bulbs are Connecticut's leading farm goods. Many Christmas trees grow there, too.

Raising dairy cows and poultry is also important. Connecticut farmers sell milk. Most of their chickens are raised to lay eggs.

Chapter 6
Seeing the Sights

Connecticut is a small state. Yet visitors find much to see and do. Tiny villages are full of history. Fun lies along the seacoast. The state's hills and forests are filled with beauty.

Western Connecticut

Lakeville is in northwestern Connecticut. The Salisbury Cannon Museum is there. The museum tells about the town's role in the Revolutionary War. Its iron forges made weapons for the colonial troops.

Litchfield is southeast of Lakeville. Colonial homes line the old village square. Many visitors

Yale University covers several blocks of New Haven. It is one of the sights to see in Connecticut.

stop at the Tapping Reeve House. This is where the first U.S. law school started in 1784.

Kent Falls State Park is west of Litchfield. Hikers walk to the waterfall. People catch fish in the stream.

Nearby is the town of Kent. It was once a great ironmaking town. Today, many visitors enjoy its shops and art galleries.

Bristol is in the west-central part of the state. The American Clock and Watch Museum is there. It has more than 3,000 timepieces.

The Connecticut Valley

Windsor Locks is in the northern valley. Bradley International Airport is outside the city. The New England Air Museum is next to the airport. This museum has 75 aircraft. They include bombers, gliders, and helicopters.

Hartford is in the middle of the state. This is the state capital. The Old State House was Connecticut's capitol building from 1796 to 1879. Today, this building is the nation's oldest state house.

Hartford also has the Science Museum of Connecticut. It has a full-size model of a whale. Visitors can walk inside the whale.

South of Hartford is Dinosaur State Park. Dinosaurs walked there millions of years ago. Today, visitors can see dinosaur tracks. They can also make plaster casts of the giant footprints.

Eastern Connecticut

Woodstock is in northeastern Connecticut. The Photomobile Model Museum is there. The museum houses scale-model boats, cars, planes, and trains. They are all powered by the sun. Visitors can drive solar-powered carts.

Storrs is southwest of Woodstock. The University of Connecticut is there. About 26,000 students attend. The University of Connecticut started as an agricultural college. It still has farm animals, but students can study many different subjects.

Norwich is in the southeastern part of the state. The Native American Burial Grounds are in this town. Uncas, the Mohegan chief, is buried there.

Along the Sound

New London is on the west bank of the Thames River. The Nathan Hale Schoolhouse is there. Hale taught school before the Revolutionary War. He was a spy for the colonists during the war. The British caught and hanged him in 1776.

Groton is across the Thames. Visitors can board the USS *Nautilus*. This was the first nuclear-powered submarine. It was built in Groton.

New Haven is west along Long Island Sound. Yale University covers several blocks in the city center. This school was founded in 1701. Today, students eat at Louis' Lunch. The first American hamburger was served there.

Bridgeport is to the west. It was home to the Greatest Show on Earth. This was Phineas T. Barnum's great circus. Today, the Barnum Museum is there. It displays a model of his three-ring circus.

Norwalk is farther west along the coast. Visitors can take a ferry to Sheffield Island. A 10-room lighthouse stands there.

Connecticut Cities

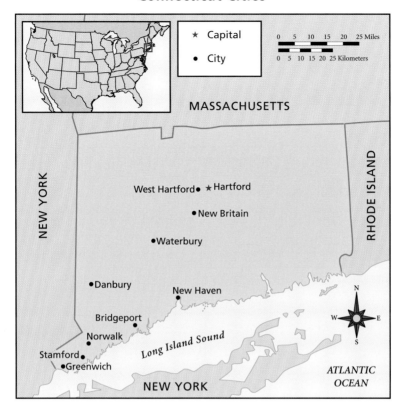

Greenwich lies on Connecticut's border with New York. It is one of the wealthiest towns in the United States. Shoppers can buy expensive cars and clothes.

The Audubon Center is also in Greenwich. Visitors can walk its 15 miles (24 kilometers) of trails. Along the way, they see many kinds of birds.

Connecticut Time Line

8000 B.C.—The first people reach Connecticut.

A.D. 1614—Adriaen Block, a Dutch explorer, finds the Connecticut Valley.

1633—English colonists move into Connecticut.

1636—Settlements in Windsor, Wethersfield, and Hartford form the Connecticut Colony.

1638—Other English settlers found the New Haven Colony.

1665—New Haven becomes part of the Connecticut Colony.

1701—Yale University is founded; Hartford and New Haven are twin capitals.

1775-1783—The colonists fight England in the Revolutionary War and win their independence.

1776—Nathan Hale is hanged as a spy by the British.

1788—Connecticut becomes the fifth state.

1817—Thomas Gallaudet starts the first school for the deaf in Hartford.

1836—Samuel Colt patents the first repeating pistol.

1864—The Travelers Insurance Company in Hartford sells the nation's first accident insurance policy.

1875—Hartford becomes the only capital of Connecticut.

1878—The world's first telephone exchange opens in New Haven.

1910—The Coast Guard Academy moves to New London.

1917—The navy builds a submarine base at Groton.

1954—The USS *Nautilus* is launched at Groton.

1965—Connecticut adopts a new state constitution.

1981—Thirman Milner is elected mayor of Hartford, becoming the first African-American mayor of a New England city.

1987—Carrie Saxon Perry is elected mayor of Hartford, becoming the first African-American woman mayor of a large U.S. city.

1989—The team from Trumbull wins the Little League World Series.

1991—Lowell P. Weicker, Jr. becomes governor; the state adopts a state income tax.

1995—The University of Connecticut's women's basketball team wins the NCAA championship.

Famous Nutmeggers

Ethan Allen (1738-1789) Leader of the Green Mountain Boys during the Revolutionary War; born in Litchfield.

Phineas T. (P. T.) Barnum (1810-1891) Showman who helped found the Ringling Brothers Barnum and Bailey Circus; born in Bethel.

Samuel Clemens (Mark Twain) (1835-1910) Author who wrote *Huckleberry Finn* and *Tom Sawyer* while living in Hartford.

Ella Grasso (1919-1981) Politician who became Connecticut's first woman governor (1975-1980); born in Windsor Locks.

Dorothy Hamill (1956-) Figure skater who won a gold medal at the 1976 Winter Olympics; born in Riverside.

Katharine Hepburn (1909-) Actress who has won four Academy Awards for best actress; born in Hartford.

Edwin Land (1909-1991) Inventor who founded the Polaroid Corporation and developed the Polaroid Land camera; born in Bridgeport.

Calvin Murphy (1948-) Pro basketball player who set free throw records; born in Norwalk.

Adam Clayton Powell (1908-1972) Minister and U.S. congressman from New York (1945-1967, 1969-1971); born in New Haven.

Israel Putnam (1718-1790) Revolutionary War general who shouted, "Don't fire until you see the whites of their eyes!" at the Battle of Bunker Hill; lived in Pomfret.

Benjamin Spock (1903-1998) Children's doctor who wrote *Baby and Child Care*; born in New Haven.

Harriet Beecher Stowe (1811-1896) Author of *Uncle Tom's Cabin*, an anti-slavery book; born in Litchfield.

Uncas (1588?-1683?) Pequot Indian who formed the Mohegan tribe and sided with the colonists in the Pequot War; born in Connecticut.

Noah Webster (1758-1843) Writer who put together *An American Dictionary of the English Language*; born in West Hartford.

Eli Whitney (1765-1825) Inventor who mass-produced rifles with interchangeable parts; set up a factory near New Haven.

Words to Know

artificial—made by humans, not by nature

cast—an exact copy made by using wet plaster that hardens

colony—a group of people who settle in a distant land but remain governed by their native country

commuter—a person who travels from home in one community to work in another community

constitution—the basic law of a country

ethnic group—people with a common culture

glider—an aircraft powered by wind rather than by a motor

humid—air that is heavy with moisture

immigrate—to come to a country to settle

insurance policy—a written agreement in which an insurance company guarantees payment in case of accident, illness, death, or property damage

manufacturing—the making of products

peddler—a person who goes door-to-door selling items

ratify—to approve a law or a constitution

reservation—land set aside for use by Native Americans

tourism—the business of providing services such as food and lodging for travelers

urban—relating to cities and large towns

To Learn More

Furstinger, Nancy. *Connecticut.* From Sea to Shining Sea. New York: Children's Press, 2002.

Girod, Christina. *Connecticut.* Thirteen Colonies. San Diego, Cal.: Lucent Books, 2001.

McNair, Sylvia. *Connecticut.* America the Beautiful. New York: Children's Press, 1999.

O'Hara, Megan, ed. *A Whaling Captain's Daughter: The Diary of Laura Jernegan, 1868-1871.* Diaries, Letters, and Memoirs. Mankato, Minn.: Blue Earth Books, 2000.

Webster, Christine. *Connecticut.* A Guide to American States. Mankato, Minn.: Weigl Publishers, 2001.

Useful Addresses

Barnum Museum
820 Main Street
Bridgeport, CT 06604

Fort Saybrook Monument Park
Saybrook Point
Route 154
Old Saybrook, CT 06475

Institute for American Indian Studies
38 Curtis Road
Washington, CT 06793

The Mark Twain House
351 Farmington Avenue
Hartford, CT 06105

Mystic Marinelife Aquarium
55 Coogan Boulevard
Mystic, CT 06355

Old State House
800 Main Street
Hartford, CT 06103

USS *Nautilus*/Submarine Force Museum
U.S. Naval Submarine Base
Route 12
Groton, CT 06349

Internet Sites

Connecticut:We're Full of Surprises
http://www.50states.com/connecti.htm

ConneCT Kids
http://www.state.ct.us

Travel.org—Connecticut
http://travel.org/conn.html

Welcome to Mystic Seaport
http://www.mystic.org

Index